Word Writers

Philippians

Denise J. Hughes

HARVEST HOUSE PUBLISHERS
EUGENE, OREGON

Cover by Connie Gabbert Design + Illustration, Bend, OR

Published in association with The Steve Laube Agency, LLC, 5025 N. Central Ave., #635, Phoenix, Arizona, 85012.

WORD WRITERS: PHILIPPIANS

Copyright © 2016 Denise J. Hughes
Published by Harvest House Publishers
Eugene, Oregon 97402
www.harvesthousepublishers.com

ISBN 978-0-7369-6847-8 (pbk.)

Printed in China

16 17 18 19 20 21 22 23 24 / RDS-JC / 10 9 8 7 6 5 4 3 2 1

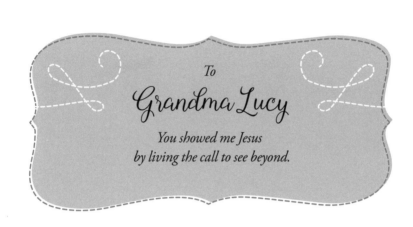

To

Grandma Lucy

You showed me Jesus
by living the call to see beyond.

Contents

Welcome to Word Writers

Welcome to Word Writers! It's truly a joy to invite you to join me on this journey through the Bible by writing the words of Scripture. Word Writers is a Bible study specially designed for individuals as well as groups. It's an inductive-plus Bible Study that makes the Bible the primary source. A traditional inductive Bible Study uses three key approaches to God's Word: *observation*, *interpretation*, and *application*. Word Writers adds a crucial fourth dimension to the Bible study experience: *saturation*—the opportunity to write the Word. Because when we write it, we remember it. So grab a few girlfriends and get together for some tea, conversation, and Word writing!

You'll notice Psalm 119:18 at the top of each new day's page, which says, "Open my eyes so that I may contemplate wonderful things from Your instruction." Let's make this our prayer every day before we begin our time in the Word. I'll be your guide through the pages of Philippians, but the Holy Spirit is our Teacher.

> When we write it, we remember it.
>
> #WordWriters

Each day of the study will begin with a short illustration that leads into the daily Scripture reading. After reading the designated passage in Philippians, you'll come to the Diving Deeper section, which asks a few questions. The first couple of questions will ask you about the biblical text (the *observation* and *interpretation* portion of the study). Space is provided for you to pause and answer these questions in your own words. Feel free to use this space to write some of your own questions too.

The next question or two will lead you to further contemplate how you can apply the truth of Scripture to your everyday life (the *application* portion of the study). Then you're invited to write the Word (the *saturation* portion of the study). Ample space is provided in the back of this book to write out the verses from Philippians you read that day. Now, depending on your Bible's translation, the verses you write for one day may end with a comma rather than a period. That's okay. I'm using the Holman Christian Standard Bible translation, but you're welcome to use the translation you're most comfortable with.

Last, we finish each day the same way we begin—with prayer. A prayer is printed at the end of each daily study. Make the words of these prayers your own, for we know when we seek Him with all our heart, we will find Him (Jeremiah 29:13).

Philippians: A Call to See Beyond

I have a special fondness for the characters A.A. Milne created in his stories about Winnie-the-Pooh. Winnie is a plain little bear who enjoys sweet honey and good companions. His friends are of the simple variety too. Piglet is Pooh's faithful friend. Always there. Always supportive. And where Piglet is a bit child-like and innocent, Owl is wise and proud. Tigger, on the other hand, is the ever-so-sanguine life of the party. He's happy and carefree and lots of fun to be around. He gets a little lost sometimes. But that's okay. He has fun while doing it. Then there's Eeyore. Sweet but somber Eeyore.

Of all Pooh's friends, we would characterize Tigger as the most joyful of the bunch. He certainly seems to come by it naturally. In fact, I've known people, and you probably have, too, who just seem to be naturally joyful people. They're generally cheerful and upbeat; it's part of their inborn temperament. I, however, am not one of them. I happen to come from a long line of Eeyores. In a good kind of way. My great-grandmother was a serious woman. As was my grand-mother and my mother. So when it comes to being serious, I come by it hon-estly. It's part of my DNA, which isn't necessarily a bad thing. When the women in my family got together, no matter what age you were, you would bring a book with you. Then we'd sit together and, well, we would read. For some that might sound like the most boring gathering imaginable, but we loved it.

So why am I talking about fictional characters from a children's story when we're about to embark on a journey through the pages of Philippians? Because the predominant theme in this short book is joy. The words *joy* and *rejoice* appear 16 times in four brief chapters. Paul's letter to the church in Philippi reads like a "personal manifesto on how to live a life full of joy."* But before we begin you must know that for many years, when I observed joyful exuberance in other people, I viewed those Tigger-like folks as wholly other—a perplexing mystery I felt certain I would never understand. The nature of their jubilant behavior eluded me.

> Joy is anchored in the unshakable belief that something good— Someone good— lies beyond our present circumstances.
>
> #WordWriters

For far too long, I misunderstood the true nature of joy. I thought it was something you are born with, something that's part of your innate personality. But Paul says in Galatians that joy is a fruit of the Spirit. A fruit, of course, starts out small and then grows full and sweet. Joy isn't automatically conferred to the naturally optimistic crowd. It's a key virtue in a Christian's life, which means it should be evident in the lives of *all* believers. Including Eeyores like me. So, being the Eeyore I am, I have taken the topic of joy very seriously, and I've made it the subject of much study.

All kidding aside, I've grown to know joy in deeper and deeper ways over time. And while we can't take a slice of joy and examine it under a microscope, we can observe the habits of joyful people, and we can cultivate joy in our own lives with greater intention. Paul's letter to the Philippians includes the steps we can take toward a life of deeper joy. The fullness of joy, however, is more than a list of dos and don'ts. Authentic joy begins with a true understanding of its meaning. True joy must reside deep within our soul, anchored in the unshakable belief that something good—Someone good—lies beyond our present circumstances.

Consider Paul's circumstances. Even though Philippians is most known for its theme of joy, Paul wrote the letter while imprisoned, not knowing if he'd be

---

* Warren Wiersbe, "Be Joyful: Even When Things Go Wrong, You Can Have Joy"—*New Testament Commentary: Philippians* (Colorado Springs, CO: David C Cook, 1974), 9.

released or executed. Paul could have easily focused on his own grim circumstances. Chained to a Roman guard 24 hours a day, no one would have blamed him if he had chosen to settle into a miserable state of gloom. Instead, Paul wrote letters of encouragement to his friends in far places, and he prayed words of thanksgiving to his Friend in high places. Paul's joy wasn't contingent upon his external circumstances, for he saw beyond his current chains.

In Philippians, Paul conveys the idea that our joy doesn't come from the here-and-now; our joy comes from the future-when. Our joy doesn't come from the events surrounding us because our joy is rooted in the future when we are face-to-face with Jesus, when we are made complete in Him. We find this repeated theme throughout the letter:

> "I am sure of this, that He who started a good work in you will carry it on to completion until *the day of Christ Jesus*" (Philippians 1:6).

> "Hold firmly to the message of life. Then I can boast *in the day of Christ* that I didn't run or labor for nothing" (Philippians 2:16).

> "*Our citizenship is in heaven*, from which we also eagerly wait" (Philippians 3:20).

> "*The Lord is near.* Don't worry about anything" (Philippians 4:5-6).

The theme of joy in Philippians cannot be separated from Paul's consistent focus on his eternal future with Christ. So as we journey through Philippians together, we'll identify the steps we can take to cultivate joy in our lives today, but all the while, we'll also recognize the growing pulse that underscores this letter: A life of deep joy comes from a heart that sees beyond the here-and-now and awaits with great hope the eternal life we'll have with Christ. Philippians is a call to see beyond. And that's something even an Eeyore like me can learn to do.

Day 1

When Women Gather

Open my eyes so that I may contemplate wonderful things from Your instruction.

PSALM 119:18

Throughout history, women have been gathering together. It's what we do. Is someone getting married? We'll throw a bridal shower. Is someone having a baby? We'll throw a baby shower. If we don't have an excuse for getting together, we'll find one. How about the park? Moms and kids and strollers. We'll call it a playdate.

It's the same at work. Do you have some papers to grade? We'll meet in the library after school and grade papers together. What about the office? We'll do lunch. What about after work? We'll call it Girls' Night Out and have dinner.

In different seasons of my life, I've enjoyed all of the above. But the most memorable gatherings I've experienced have centered on the Word. Whether it's Tuesday evening in the sanctuary or Saturday morning in a friend's living room, when women come together to grow deeper in their relationship with God, something special happens. Hearts connect. Friendships form. Bonds deepen. And lives are changed.

The book of Philippians is a prime example of this truth. In the Roman colony of Philippi, there wasn't a synagogue in town, which meant there probably weren't enough Jewish men in the area for a synagogue. Yet every Sabbath a few women would make their way to the river, and together they would pray and sing and worship. Something about this small band of women caught God's eye, too, for He stopped the apostle Paul from traveling any farther into Asia. In a dream, Paul saw a man beckoning him to cross the Aegean Sea and visit the province of Macedonia—part of what we call Greece—which is where Philippi was located.

Read Acts 16:6-15 and Philippians 1:1-2

Paul obeys God's command at once, and when he reaches the city of Philippi, he hears about the women who gather by the river to pray. So he goes to them and preaches the cross of Christ. Lydia, a wealthy woman who sells purple linens, listens with rapt attention, her heart wide open to receive the Truth. Lydia and her whole household are baptized that same day. And the first church in Europe begins. This church will eventually grow to become a core group of believers, influencing the entire region for Christ. That's what can happen when women gather.

> When women come together to grow in their relationship with God, hearts connect, friendships form, and lives are changed.
>
> #WordWriters

Years later, while sitting in chains and waiting for his trial in Rome, Paul writes a letter to his dear friends in Philippi. The church then shares his letter with everyone. In time, this personal letter from their mentor will be inducted into the canon of Holy Scripture. The book of Philippians is the subsequent fruit born of a few women. Lydia and her friends serve as beautiful examples of what can happen when women gather to pray and worship and study the Scriptures. That's my prayer for us. The world may be a different place today, but our God is the same. When women gather, He sees, He knows, and I dare say, He smiles.

----------------- *Diving Deeper* -----------------

Who does Paul mention in his greeting to the saints in Philippi?

The fact that Paul includes the "overseers and deacons" in Philippi indicates that the church had not only grown in size, but it had also established some order. Are you familiar with your local church's organizational structure? Does your church have elders or deacons in addition to the church staff? Write their names in the space below so you begin to pray for those in leadership.

Whether this is your first Bible study or your hundredth, God's Word is alive, and He continues to speak through His Word today. God always has something new for us when we go to Him to learn from His Word. What do you hope to learn from your time in Philippians?

The first step toward a life of deeper joy is participating in community with other believers. Do you have a group of friends you can journey with? Is there someone you could invite to journey with you through Philippians?

Like Lydia and her friends, we have the dear privilege of coming together to worship God through prayer and the study of His Word. Together, we can savor the words of Scripture by writing them down. So let's grab our favorite pens and begin by writing Philippians 1:1-2.

Prayer: Thank You, Lord, for godly women who serve as beautiful examples of what can happen when women gather. Help me to grow and become that kind of woman. I pray that as I read through and write out the words of Philippians, the Holy Spirit will teach me and reveal Truth to me. I give this time to You. For You are good and true. Amen.

A Call to See Beyond
~ with gratitude and joy ~

In his letter to the Philippians, Paul paves the path toward a life of deeper joy. As we saw on Day 1, the first step on the path to deeper joy is participating in community with other believers. The second step on the path to deeper joy is remembering with gratitude the people who have shown us kindness along life's journey. Paul models for us the importance of remembering those who have been the hands and feet of Jesus to us in times of great need, and he teaches us by example to give thanks for the many ways we've been carried through a difficult season.

Partners in Grace

Open my eyes so that I may contemplate wonderful things from Your instruction.

PSALM 119:18

One of my earliest teaching jobs involved a one-hour commute each way—without traffic. But I live in the greater Los Angeles area, so there's always traffic. My commute wasn't kind to my aging Dodge sedan, either. Every morning she groaned of better days. I searched for an apartment close to the school where I taught, but I couldn't find anything in my budget. Then the worst thing possible happened. Well, maybe not the *worst* thing, but it managed to derail my life plenty good all the same. My car stopped working, and the mechanic said I'd need $3,000 to fix the transmission. I barely had enough for gas.

The price of that transmission was a small fortune, especially to my young twentysomething self. I sold what little of value I had and scraped together what little cash I could. But it still wasn't enough. Yet I needed my car working so I could keep working. So I did the only thing I knew to do. I gave my landlord my notice, paid my last month's rent, and moved what few things I owned into a small storage unit. A friend let me sleep on her couch while I used my next paycheck to cobble together the amount I needed to repair my car.

With a fixed transmission, I continued my long commute to and from work each day, but I was too embarrassed to tell anyone at school I was basically homeless. Then after school one day, a teacher from down the hall, Mrs. Larson, asked me where I lived. I told her I was staying with a friend, which was true, but her eyes widened when I told her where I was commuting from. Mrs. Larson said her children were grown and she lived alone with her husband in a large house with several empty bedrooms. She invited me to live with her for a while. I accepted her gracious offer, and for the next two months I stayed with her. She insisted that I not pay any rent. I was her guest. This allowed me to save my next couple of paychecks for a deposit on a nearby apartment. I will never forget Mrs. Larson's kindness and generosity. She helped me during a season of my life when I didn't have anyone else to turn to.

When Paul was nearing the end of his earthly life, he found himself imprisoned in Rome. He wasn't homeless, but as a prisoner, he likely wasn't able to work to support himself either, not as he had during his earlier years in ministry. Imagine the gratitude Paul must have felt when his old friend Epaphroditus appeared on his doorstep with a huge financial gift from the church in Philippi.

Read Philippians 1:3-7

Every time Paul remembers his friends in Philippi, he's filled with joy as he thanks God for them. Because a thank-full heart is a joy-full heart. Paul's letter to them is really a thank-you note for their kind generosity. He calls them his partners in grace. Every time I think of Mrs. Larson, I thank God for her. And when I moved into my own apartment, I wrote a long thank-you note to her.

> Our past cannot dictate our future. God is in the business of transforming lives.
>
> #WordWriters

Though Philippians is brief, it is full of rich truth. One such truth is Paul's assurance that God is faithful to finish the good work He has already started in us. Our past cannot dictate our future. God is in the business of transforming lives. Once we go to Him with surrendered hearts, He begins His holy work inside us, fashioning us more and more into His likeness. Lydia and the other women who gathered by the river are not the same as they were when they first met Paul. They have grown and matured in Christ and will continue to do so until they meet Jesus face-to-face. The same is true of us. What God has begun in our lives, He will finish.

Almost two decades have passed since I was a young twentysomething without a place to live. Years later, when I was sitting at my own kitchen table writing addresses on my wedding invitations, I wrote Mrs. Larson's address on an envelope from memory, her address having once been my address. Mrs. Larson and her husband traveled far to attend my wedding. No matter the years that have passed, I am filled with joy when I think of her.

Diving Deeper

When Paul prayed for the Philippians, why did joy fill his heart?

In addition to thanking his friends, what other encouragement does Paul give them?

Have you ever had a Mrs. Larson in your life? Someone who came alongside you during a trying time? Have you written a thank-you note to this person?

Paul's joy increased each time he prayed for his friends. Do you have friends you're committed to praying for on a regular basis? Who can you begin praying for today?

Write out the words of Philippians 1:3-7, and as you do, read each word aloud. This is how the ancient scribes used to copy Scripture, with their hands and their voices. Then thank God for the people He's brought into your life.

Prayer: Thank You, Lord, for caring for my physical needs as well as my spiritual needs. Thank You for bringing generous people into my life. Help me to become the kind of person who responds to the needs of those around me. Help me to become Your hands and feet. Amen.

Faithful to the End

Open my eyes so that I may contemplate wonderful things from Your instruction.

PSALM 119:18

On the outskirts of Pasadena is this little café known for its chicken potpies. The plaid-covered booths are faded and the rest of the décor looks like it's straight out of a 1970s movie. But the kitchen is clean, the atmosphere warm, and the chicken potpies are out of this world. My husband, Jeff, first took me there when we were dating, and we've been going back ever since.

Every time we go there for dinner, we're usually the youngest patrons in the restaurant by at least two or three decades. We love it. We always feel like we're in a time warp, and we've come to think of it as a picture of what we want to be doing years from now—sitting in an old booth at a much-loved café, enjoying our meal and each other's company.

We love watching the other folks in the restaurant too. There's always a couple or two, sitting side by side rather than across from each other, and they're eating off each other's plates. They've known each other so long and they know each other so well that they don't even need to ask anymore. He knows she doesn't want her peas, so he scoops them up, while she knows he can't have salt on his mashed potatoes, so she slides the saltshaker to the far end of the table. Their meal together is like a well-choreographed dance.

While sharing a chicken potpie, Jeff and I capture real-life scenes of enduring love that are better than anything Hollywood could ever dream up. Most movies with a romantic plot typically depict the courtship, the young-and-in-love couple who finally overcome all odds to be together. Once they're actually together, though, the movie ends. But in real life, that's when real love begins.

Real love is rooted in history, in shared experiences. Real love stands by you through painful circumstances, just as the Philippians stood by Paul and Silas when they were beaten and thrown into jail unjustly.

Read Acts 16:16–24 and Philippians 1:8–11

Real love is more than a deep feeling or connection between two people. That can be part of it, but when Paul prayed for the Philippians, he didn't pray their love would grow deeper in feeling. He prayed their love would grow in knowledge and discernment. Today, we don't hear the words *love, knowledge,* and *discernment* used much in the same sentence. The world would tell us love is blind. But real love isn't blind. Real love sees all and knows all and chooses to love anyway. Real love is unconditional. Real love serves and protects. Real love is demonstrated when we make sacrifices for the one we've committed our hearts to. This is how enduring love lasts.

> Real love isn't blind. Real love sees all and knows all and chooses to love anyway.
>
> #WordWriters

Paul's words make sense, for when we grow in true knowledge and discernment, we also grow in love. And when we grow in love, we grow in all the other fruit of the Spirit as well. This is the next step for cultivating a life of deeper joy: growing in love for one another.

Diving Deeper

Why does Paul pray their love will keep on growing in knowledge and discernment?

Why is it important to "approve the things that are superior" or "discern what is best"?

When have you seen an example of enduring love? What made this moment unique?

Why is real love rooted in a shared history? Which friends do you have a long history with?

As we write out Philippians 1:8-11, let's ask God to show us one person in our lives who could use a little encouragement today. Then let's reach out with a phone call to say we're thinking of them.

Prayer: Thank You, Lord, for encouraging us to keep growing in love, in knowledge, and in discernment. Help me to become the kind of person others can count on. Deepen my love for others as I continue to get to know in deeper ways the beautiful people You have placed in my life. May Your kindness and steadfastness become the hallmark of my heart. Amen.

A Call to See Beyond
~ our circumstances and our critics ~

If we live long enough, we're bound to experience a few less-than-desirable circumstances. We're also sure to encounter at least a few critics. It's inevitable. Why? Because the enemy of our soul seeks to destroy all that is good. So we shouldn't be surprised when we hear alarming news of someone gloating over another person's misfortune. It's a sad reality. But as believers in Christ, we're called to a higher standard. With our hope firmly in Christ, and with the assurance of His unique purpose for our lives, we're free to rejoice over another person's success. We're also able to overcome negative criticism because we know who the real Judge is. And what He thinks is what really matters.

Living with Limits

Open my eyes so that I may contemplate wonderful things from Your instruction.

PSALM 119:18

If you live in California, then you know earthquakes come with the territory. My first big earthquake was a 7.1 on the Richter scale at 3:00 in the morning. At first I dreamt I was lying on a raft, enjoying a lazy afternoon on a gently rolling lake, but I soon awoke to the sound of glass dishes clattering in the cupboards. The earth seemed to growl as the walls of my home swayed back and forth. I jumped out of bed and ran to my daughter's bedroom. Simone was only five years old at the time, and I carried her from her bed to the hallway, where we huddled under the doorway together. The whole time I wondered, *Is this the big one?*

It wasn't. Fortunately, the epicenter was located in the desert. Despite its force, minimal damage was done. Once the world quit moving beneath us, Simone asked, "Mommy, what was *that?*"

"That was an earthquake, honey."

But Simone replied matter-of-factly, "No, Mommy. That's not an earthquake. When Miss Davis rings a funny bell at school and we all get under the table, *that's* an earthquake."

I couldn't help but chuckle at her perspective. She only knew the term *earthquake* because of safety drills at school. In today's reading, Paul talks about his imprisonment, and his friends in Philippi will remember the time he was imprisoned in their city as well. Back in Philippi, a great earthquake had once flung the prison doors wide open for Paul.

Read Acts 16:25-40 and Philippians 1:12-14

In Philippi, Paul had been thrown into prison with his friend Silas. With their backs bloodied from a beating, they actually chose to sing hymns of praise to God, which defied all reason considering their condition. Then, before night's end, an earthquake shook their chains loose and the gates of the prison flew open. But once again, their actions defied logic, for they didn't take advantage of the easy escape in front of them. They stayed, much to the relief of the sleeping guard. In the end, the guard's soul was saved, along with his entire household. They probably joined the church Paul started with Lydia and the others.

Now, years later, Paul finds himself imprisoned again—this time in Rome, after two previous years of imprisonment in Caesarea. If I were Paul, I would be wondering why God wasn't sending another earthquake to set me free. After all, He did it once, and He could do it again. So why wasn't He? What was He waiting for?

But Paul's perspective is atypical. He sees a different picture. He recognizes his influence among the imperial guard. Christ is being preached to all the guards who wouldn't ordinarily have come within proximity of Paul otherwise. So Paul rejoices not only in the guards who have believed the gospel message, but also because the other Christians in the area have grown more confident in their own preaching! Paul embraces his limitations as a prisoner and gladly accepts whatever purview the Lord allows him. This is the next step in cultivating a life of deeper joy: accepting the limits of our situation while trusting the Lord to work beyond them. When we live within our limits, we discover a joy beyond our understanding.

We discover joy as we accept the limits of our situation and trust the Lord to work beyond them.

#WordWriters

Diving Deeper

Why does Paul believe his imprisonment has actually served to advance the gospel?

How are the other Christians in the area responding to Paul's imprisonment?

When have you experienced severe limitations, either physically, financially, or situationally? What did you learn from this experience?

When have you wondered why the Lord seemed to take a long time to move in a situation and relieve the suffering? Why does God seem to move so slowly sometimes? What might He be trying to show you in the meantime?

Let's write out Philippians 1:12-14, asking God to help us grow in grace as we learn to accept certain limitations in our lives.

Prayer: Thank You, Lord, for moving when You know the time is right. Forgive me when I allow impatience to overtake me and I become anxious for You to move faster. Help me to see things the way You see them, and help me to trust You when I fail to see anything at all. I know You're trustworthy, yet I also know I still have room in my heart to grow in my trust in You. Amen.

Living with Goodwill

Open my eyes so that I may contemplate wonderful things from Your instruction.

PSALM 119:18

My mom says there are two kinds of people in the world: skunks and turtles. When skunks get upset, they make a big stink, and everybody knows about it for miles around. But when turtles get upset, they quietly pull into their shell. Most people might not even notice.

I'm a turtle. That's not to say I don't ever have skunk-ish moments. I do. But for the most part, whenever I'm sad or hurt or angry, I withdraw. I pull into my shell. The deeper the hurt, the more distant I become.

It's tempting to label the skunks as more destructive, and perhaps outwardly they are. But turtles can be just as destructive inwardly. I may not get together with others to gossip about whatever situation is bothering me, and I may not engage in a harsh exchange of words, but when I'm hurting I tend to cope by nursing a grudge and eating too many French fries.

These may sound like mild offenses, but in reality, my withdrawal is the same as choosing not to love certain people who have hurt me. And let's face it, I'm only hurting myself with all those French fries!

The two greatest commandments are to love God and love others (Matthew 22:37-39). I'm cool with the "loving God" part. It's the "loving others" part that can be a challenge, especially when someone has been particularly hurtful. In today's reading, we observe how Paul responds to a hurtful situation.

Read Philippians 1:15-20

As if being imprisoned isn't enough, a group of believers in Rome wish Paul ill. It's considered a cultural source of shame for anyone to be imprisoned, no matter the reason, and these believers are actually gloating over Paul's imprisonment. Not unbelievers. Believers! It's one thing to feel the disdain of an unbeliever, but it's quite another thing altogether to be the recipient of ill will from someone in the body of Christ, much less a whole group of them! Division among the believers in Rome clearly exists.

Few things grieve God's heart like division in the church. And few things cause division more than competition. The fruit of competition in ministry always leads to division, yet we're called to live in unity as one body with one hope (see Ephesians 4:3-6). Some of the believers in Rome, however, are competing with Paul, which sounds silly two thousand years later. Why would anyone want to compete with the apostle? We're on the same side! We want to reach hurting souls with the good news of Jesus Christ! But Paul knew their motives. They were insincere, which is another reason he urged the Philippians earlier in his letter to grow in knowledge and discernment (1:9). We must be wise and discerning, for we never know what motives might be lurking beneath the surface. Sometimes even our own motives surprise us.

> When we serve God with right motives and a pure heart, we rejoice over the success of others.
>
> #WordWriters

There's one telltale sign of a person serving with pure motives: joy. A person serving God with right motives and a pure heart rejoices over the success of others and mourns when others experience hurt and disappointment. A pure heart never gloats over another person's misfortune. How does Paul respond to the group of believers in Rome who want to see his demise? He's neither a skunk nor a turtle. Rather, he rejoices that Christ is being proclaimed. This is the next step in cultivating a life of deeper joy: rejoicing over the success of others.

Diving Deeper

As others rejoice over Paul's imprisonment, what matters most to Paul?

How does Paul choose to respond to such adversity?

When have you struggled to rejoice over someone else's success? (We've probably all been there.) How were you able to work through the negative emotion until you could genuinely rejoice over their success?

Is someone in your life currently trying for something, such as a new job, a new opportunity, or even a new baby? How can you begin to pray for God's blessing over that person's life?

While writing out Philippians 1:15-20, ask God to enlarge your heart so you can always rejoice over the success of others.

Prayer: Thank You, Lord, for always having goodwill toward me. Help me to forgive those who might have ill will toward me. Help me to see them as You see them. Please ferret out my heart's true motives and purify my heart so I might always rejoice over the success of others. May I be the kind of person who truly loves to advocate for other people. Amen.

A Call to See Beyond
~ the here-and-now ~

The first chapter of Philippians is like a crescendo, the pulse steadily growing, until Paul reaches his ultimate message: "For to me, to live is Christ and to die is gain" (1:21 NIV). Nothing else matters to Paul. He wants to be with Jesus more than anything. His focus isn't on the here-and-now. His focus is on being with Christ. He isn't fretting over the people in Rome who are gloating over his imprisonment. He's not even worrying about whether he'll be executed by Nero. All of that pales in comparison to spending eternity with Jesus. Paul is willing to stay on earth longer, for the sake of others. And for as long as he's alive, he wants to live his life for the sake of Christ.

For the Sake of Others

Open my eyes so that I may contemplate wonderful things from Your instruction.

PSALM 119:18

My daughter Simone reads the acceptance letters again. Her top two college choices have each accepted her application and offered her a generous scholarship. Now she must decide. Both universities are great. So which school should she attend? There isn't a clear-cut answer. She's torn.

Perhaps you've felt torn at a time in your life, too, whether it was two school offers or two job openings or two ministry opportunities. Yet you could only choose one. In today's reading, Paul feels torn. Part of him would rather depart to be with Christ right now. But the other part of him thinks it might be better, for the sake of others, to remain on earth a little longer, enduring more hardship, so he can continue to preach Christ. His dilemma might sound a little morose, but he's waiting for trial and he knows his execution is a real possibility.

In the end he believes he should stay so he can reach more souls with the message of Christ's freedom. His words here become the apex of his letter: "For to me, to live is Christ and to die is gain" (1:21 NIV). Paul is at peace no matter the outcome.

Read Philippians 1:21-26

Finishing well is the hallmark of mature believers, and it's important to Paul that he finishes well, whether that means departing to be with Christ now or later. Paul is committed to whatever path God has for him.

Until we reach the ultimate "finish line" at the end of our lives, we experience other finishes along life's journey. And when we do, we have an important choice to make. When leaving a job, a volunteer position, or a ministry leadership role to pursue a new adventure somewhere else, it's important that we finish well. To leave well is to love well. This is how we honor those who have been a part of our lives. This is how we build lasting ties, the kind that will span time and distance. When we don't leave well, we can leave a wake of confusion, or even hurt, behind us. Leaving well frees us to love those who become a part of our past as well as those who become a part of our future. For we take our character with us everywhere we go. And how we say "good-bye" says a lot about who we are. So when we're facing an important decision, like which college to attend or which job to take, it's equally important that we choose to leave our current place under positive conditions whenever possible. This is the next step in cultivating a life of deeper joy: finishing each season of life in a way that honors others.

> How we say good-bye says a lot about who we are. Remember: To leave well is to love well.
>
> #WordWriters

Diving Deeper

What does Paul mean when he says living here a little longer means more fruitful work?

Which does Paul say is better? Staying with the believers on earth? Or departing to be with Christ?

When have you felt torn between two possibilities? What did you choose?

Whenever we face a difficult decision, how can we be assured that we're making the right decision?

As you write out Philippians 1:21-26, thank God for the peace He imparts when we are walking forward on the path He's laid out for us.

Prayer: Thank You, Lord, for being with me when I face decisions. Thank You for guiding me with Your wisdom. And thank You for giving me a deep peace when I'm walking in the direction You would have me go. Help me to be the kind of person who not only makes decisions with wisdom, but also finishes well. Amen.

For the Sake of Christ

Open my eyes so that I may contemplate wonderful things from Your instruction.
PSALM 119:18

When it comes to our identity, we control only a few things. For instance, we can't choose our genetic makeup or where we were born or what family we were raised in. We don't even choose our names. I'm Denise, a redhead from a small farming town in Northern California. I did not choose these parts of my identity, but they are still true of me. I did, however, choose other parts of my identity, the most important parts. I'm a follower of Christ, a wife, a mom, a teacher, and a writer.

Now, when it comes to integrity, we always have a choice. But what is integrity? Integrity means wholeness, an undivided state of being. Back in middle-school math, we're told an *integer* is a whole number, not a fraction. And the word *integrate* means to bring multiple parts together to form a whole.

Integer. Integrate. Integrity.

Obviously, these three words come from the same root word. To be a person of integrity is to integrate the various parts of our identity into one whole person—who we are at home, at work, at school, at church, at the grocery store, and everywhere else. If I behave differently in these various places, then I am not a person of integrity. But if I'm consistent in how I talk and how I treat others, no matter where I am, then I become a person of integrity.

And that's the identity I want.

> Harmony among believers is paramount to gospel living.
>
> #WordWriters

Read Philippians 1:27–30

As a Roman colony, the colonists of Philippi can boast of their Roman citizenship. Even though they aren't actually in Rome, they have the same rights as the citizens of Rome. This is a huge part of their identity. At the same time, a believer's citizenship is in heaven, so Paul instructs all of the Philippians to live as citizens of heaven, in a manner worthy of the gospel, which includes living in unity with other believers. Harmony among believers is paramount to gospel living. This is yet another step in cultivating a life of deeper joy: living in harmony with others. But true harmony is possible only when believers are walking in integrity, when their manner of being is consistent wherever they go.

Diving Deeper

What does Paul mean when he says to "live your life in a manner worthy of the gospel" (1:27)?

Why is it important that believers stand firm "in one spirit, with one mind" (1:27)?

Which parts of your identity were you born with? Which parts of your identity did you choose?

Why does Paul say it's a privilege for believers to suffer for Christ? What does "suffering for Christ" mean in your life?

Let's write out Philippians 1:27-30, thanking God for the parts of our identity He chose for us.

Prayer: Thank You, Lord, for choosing the time and place for me to be born. Thank You for fashioning me in Your image. Help me to embrace the parts of my identity I didn't choose for myself. Help me to trust that You have a plan and a purpose for making me who I am. Help me to live out this purpose for the sake of Christ, for Your glory. Amen.

A Call to See Beyond
~ our own interests ~

In chapter 2, Paul calls believers to see beyond their own interests and look to the interests of others (2:4). Then he gives four examples for the Philippians to follow. The first and greatest example is, of course, Jesus. He is the One we want to emulate above all. Then Paul gives three more examples of regular people who have answered the call, whose footsteps we can follow: Paul, Timothy, and Epaphroditus. So while we look at these godly examples in chapter 2, we'll also discuss some of the ways that we, too, can become people who look to the interests of others.

Day 8

Looking Out for Others

Open my eyes so that I may contemplate wonderful things from Your instruction.

PSALM 119:18

While chasing our two-year-old son, I notice my husband, Jeff, standing very still at the living room window. On my second pass through the living room, I see Jeff putting his shoes back on. But he'd only been home from work a few minutes.

"Where are you going?"

"The garbage trucks came by yesterday," he says, "but Kay's trash cans are still at the curb."

Kay is our next-door neighbor, but Jeff says this with a sense of urgency I fail to understand.

"That's nice, honey, but could you bring them in for her *after* you help me get this boy in the bathtub?"

"Denise, she has MS, remember? Maybe the cans are still out there because she's having one of those spells. Maybe she needs help."

Here I am, the person who's in this house every minute of every day, yet I'm not the one who notices our neighbor's trash cans still sitting on the street. I wrangle my squirmy boy into my arms and manage to follow Jeff outside. I wait, almost as impatiently as my two-year-old, while he knocks on our neighbor's door. After a few minutes of no response, I assume she's not home—even though her car is in the driveway.

"Come on, Jeff. Let's get her cans for her and go home." But Jeff insists on giving Kay more time.

"She has to move slowly," he says, "so we have to give her extra time to answer the door."

I realize he's right. Again. A few moments later, Kay opens her door. She looks tired, but she assures us she's fine. She's just having a rough couple of days physically. We exchange numbers, though, so she can call us if she ever needs anything.

Read Philippians 2:1-4

Years have passed since I followed Jeff next door, but I learned an important lesson that day. We have a responsibility to our neighbors, in a real and tangible sense. Jeff was much more attuned to this need than I was.

Paul kicks off chapter 2 with a statement that acts as a hanger, for the rest of the chapter will hang on these two verses: "Do nothing out of selfish ambition or vain conceit. Rather, in humility value others above yourselves, not looking to your own interests but each of you to the interests of the others" (2:3-4 NIV). Not only is this the right thing to do, but it's also the next step in cultivating a life of deeper joy: looking to the interests of others. Besides, when we're looking out for others, we can trust that God is looking out for us.

> As we're looking out for others, we can trust that God is also looking out for us.
>
> #WordWriters

Diving Deeper

The word *if* appears four times in the first verse. What does each *if* statement ask us to do, then, in the second verse?

Paul just finished talking about the people in Rome who were competing with him in ministry (1:15-17). So now he offers the antithesis by saying we should do nothing out of rivalry (HCSB) or selfish ambition (ESV, NIV), but instead we should have humility. Why are competition and humility incompatible?

How well do you know your neighbors? What are some ways you could be a blessing to them?

Beyond your neighbors, what are some ways you can look to the interests of the people you encounter throughout your day?

As you write out Philippians 2:1-4, ask God to show you some ways you can be a blessing to the people you come across every day.

Prayer: Thank You, Lord, for the way You look out for me, even in ways I probably can't see. Forgive me when I'm too caught up in my own interests. Help me to look to other people's interests and to trust You with mine. Replace my heart of selfish ambition with a heart of humility. And lead me in Your footsteps. Amen.

What Love Looks Like

Open my eyes so that I may contemplate wonderful things from Your instruction.

PSALM 119:18

The popular picture book *Guess How Much I Love You* by Sam McBratney tells of a father's love. Little Nutbrown Hare stretches out his arms as far as they can reach and says, "I love you this much." But his father, Big Nutbrown Hare, stretches his arms even wider and says, "But I love you this much."

So it goes throughout the story, with Little Nutbrown Hare trying to think of bigger and bigger ways to express his love for his dad. Finally, Little Nutbrown Hare thinks of the farthest place possible and says, "I love you right up to the moon." With that, he closes his eyes and falls asleep. Then father Nutbrown Hare whispers, "I love you right up to the moon—and back."

I love you. Three little words. One big meaning. I tell my kids I love them every day. And we can play the same game Little Nutbrown Hare played with his father, but at the end of the day our words must be accompanied by our actions. This is how God the Father showed His love for us. He told us, over and over throughout the Old Testament, how much He loves us.

Then the day came when He showed us how much He loves us. God the Son left the glory of heaven and came to earth as a helpless infant, demonstrating the epitome of humility. Jesus grew to adulthood in both poverty and obscurity, demonstrating a heart of modesty. Then He served others selflessly for years, only to die the most undignified death—execution by crucifixion. But He defied death and

> Through Jesus' life, death, and resurrection, God has said to us all, "I love you from heaven to earth—and back."
>
> #WordWriters

rose again. After spending some time with His disciples, friends, and family, He returned to His Father's side in heaven so He could send the Holy Spirit.

In this way, God has said to us all, "I love you from heaven to earth—and back."

Read Philippians 2:5-8

Today's passage begins what is known as the Hymn of Christ (Philippians 2:5-11). We cannot fully grasp what Jesus gave up when He left heaven to be with us, to be one of us. We cannot fully comprehend the utter degradation He endured on the cross. But when we meditate on Paul's words here in chapter 2, we catch a shadow of a glimpse. God, the All-Powerful, Magnificent, and Holy One. He lowered Himself below His own creatures. He subjected Himself to the mockery of the very people He created. We can't begin to fathom the disgrace and shame He bore so we wouldn't have to. All because He loves us. From heaven to earth—and back.

This is what Love looks like. Real love makes real sacrifices. And if we're to know the same love and the same joy, then we, too, will take the next step: sacrificing for the sake of others.

Diving Deeper

Whose attitude (or mind-set) should we emulate?

When Jesus left heaven and came to earth, what form (or nature) did He take on?

What did Jesus become obedient to?

It's unlikely that any of us will ever face a death by crucifixion. But what are some of the ways we can follow in Christ's footsteps as this passage portrays? In other words, what are some of the sacrifices we can make for the sake of others?

Today let's write out Philippians 2:5-8, the first part of the Hymn of Christ. Write the words slowly, pondering each phrase. Tomorrow we'll write out the rest. In this way, we will devote two full days to this important passage of Scripture.

Prayer: Thank You, Lord, for leaving the beauty and glory of heaven and coming to earth, to take on the nature of a humble servant. You did this for me. To reconcile me back to You. I may never fully know what it really cost You, but I want to spend the rest of my days thanking You. I'm so grateful for the grace You've given me. Amen.

Day 10

What Heaven Sounds Like

Open my eyes so that I may contemplate wonderful things from Your instruction.

PSALM 119:18

The man in uniform studies my passport with a serious furrow to his brow. His consternation unsettles me, but then he finally lets me through. On the other side of customs, I find my team and we pile into an old rented van. Miles and miles of dirt roads lead us deep into the countryside, where we meet a pastor who then guides us to another camp several more hours away. More bumpy roads. More queasy tummies.

Finally, we arrive at our destination. The warmest of welcomes greets us. With hugs and tears, these strangers act like they're family. In a sense, I realize, they are. We're brothers and sisters, united in Christ, with the same Father in heaven. The people press in all around us as a spontaneous worship service erupts. My friends and I look at each other with a sort of helplessness. We know neither the language nor the tune to join in, yet we bask in His presence while watching a persecuted people praise the Lord. First one song. Then another.

The sweetest kind of joy fills the place as yet a third melody begins. A foreign familiarity draws us, something to the tune of "This Is the Day." Then we realize, hey, we know this song too!

This is the day that the Lord has made. I will rejoice and be glad in it.

Without delay, we sing the same song but in English. To my surprise, the different syllables and pronunciations of our languages don't clash. We're worshipping the same God in the same spirit and the same truth. In two different languages! If ever a foretaste of heaven could be found on earth, it's in this moment.

See beyond...our own interests • 55

Read Philippians 2:9-11

During one particularly hectic season of my life, I didn't have a Bible study or a Bible reading plan to follow, and I found myself floundering during any "quiet time" I could muster. So I settled on Philippians 2:9-11. I read it every day. In the morning after I woke up. While waiting in the car line to pick up my kids at school. And at night before bed. As I meditated on this passage, I committed the words to memory. This is one of the steps we can take toward cultivating a life of deeper joy: committing Scripture to memory.

Ever since that time, if I'm tempted to skip a day when I "don't have the time" to read God's Word, I pause for a moment, instead, to reread Philippians 2:9-11. Because the truths contained in these few verses tap the reaches beyond our finite understanding. Jesus embraced the deepest humility, and God bestowed on Him the highest glory. And one day every knee will bow and every tongue confess that Jesus Christ is Lord.

> Jesus embraced the deepest humility, and God bestowed on Him the highest glory.
>
> #WordWriters

I can hear it already. People from every nation in every language will worship together in one magnificent choir, and it won't clash. It will be the most harmonious symphony for all eternity.

Diving Deeper

How does Paul describe the name God gave to His Son?

In verse 10, what does Paul mean when he says "every knee will bow—of those who are in heaven and on earth and under the earth"?

How will heaven be a picture of true diversity? Does your circle of friends reflect the same? Does your church?

What are some ways you can humble yourself in your day-to-day living?

Write out Philippians 2:9-11, the remainder of the Hymn of Christ. As you do, exalt His name in the highest of praise.

Prayer: Jesus, Your name is above every name. You are exalted above the heavens and the earth. And with my tongue, I will praise You and worship You. For You are my Savior, my Redeemer, and my Lord. You are infinitely worthy of all glory and honor. Amen.

A Call to See Beyond
~ what others might miss ~

Heroes are in our midst—difference makers we might miss. They aren't preaching powerful sermons or singing spectacular solos. They're hidden among our pews, serving behind the scenes. They're hugging kids and welcoming strangers. When I think of the people who have made the biggest impact in my life, I notice they all have the same thing in common: They live humble lives, faithfully completing the task the Lord has given them. As we look more closely at the lives of Paul, Timothy, and Epaphroditus, let us also consider the "hidden heroes" among us and how we can become one of them.

Day 11

Shining with Joy

Open my eyes so that I may contemplate wonderful things from Your instruction.

PSALM 119:18

At choir rehearsal one night, the worship pastor announces that the Worship and Creative Arts Department is going to put on *Joseph and the Amazing Technicolor Dreamcoat*. It's a Broadway-style musical, based on the story of Joseph in Genesis 37–47, and the whole choir is invited to participate in the cast. (Yeah, it's a mega church, and we're in L.A.) For the next few months, we learn the songs and choreography, we wrestle with colorful costumes, and we slather on enough stage makeup to scare any poor toddler we happen upon.

On opening night, I double-check that I have everything I need for each scene. Costumes, shoes, props. Everything I need is in place. Everything except the pom-poms, because at one point in the show, I don't have enough time to run backstage to grab the pom-poms for the next scene. So the props manager, Allison, stands just behind the curtain, holding my pom-poms for me. All I have to do is step behind the curtain, take the pom-poms from Allison, and a second later I'm back on stage, just in time. As the narrator sings *Red!* I'm supposed to hold up the red pom-pom, and when she sings *Yellow!* I lift up the yellow pom-pom. It's all perfectly choreographed with the lyrics about Joseph's coat.

In the final scene of the show, Jacob and Joseph are reunited, and the whole cast takes a grand bow. While I'm bowing, I see Allison behind the stage curtain. She's beaming with joy. She looks so pleased that everything went off without a hitch. I know Allison helps other cast members, too, the same way she

> We find the deepest delight when we serve in hidden ways.
>
> #WordWriters

• 59 •

helps me with my pom-poms. We all know the show could not go on without her. She's like the wizard in Oz behind the curtain, making all the stage magic happen.

All of a sudden I'm sad because she isn't taking a bow on stage with the rest of us. The applause is as much for her as for those of us on stage. If anything, she's worked harder than any of us. But Allison doesn't look sad. She looks positively content, and I can't help but wonder: What is that like? Working behind the curtain? Holding someone else's pom-poms? And never receiving any applause? Would I be as content doing the same?

Read Philippians 2:12–16

Paul says we should shine like stars. But we don't have to put ourselves on a stage, under a spotlight, to shine. We simply need to live a life that follows in Christ's footsteps. We humble ourselves. We serve others. We complete the tasks we're given without grumbling or complaining. We do the things most people would wince at. And we do them with a glad heart. We don't need to tell anyone about them, either.

As a twentysomething on stage, I struggled to understand Allison's joy in serving behind the scenes. I thought the real joy was out on stage, taking bows under bright lights. But Allison knew something I didn't: We find the deepest delight when we serve in hidden ways. And when we serve others with a humble heart, our lives will shine with a joy the world might not understand. Allison is one of my "hidden heroes," for she taught me the next step toward a life of deeper joy: serving in hidden ways.

---------------------------- *Diving Deeper* ----------------------------

Paul says we should work out our own salvation with fear and trembling (2:12). Now, he doesn't mean we can earn our salvation through good works; he simply means once we're Christ-followers, serving others and doing good works will be a natural outpouring of what God has already poured into us. What are some of the ways you can work out your own salvation?

Who enables us to desire God's good purpose for our lives?

When have you completed a task with grumbling and complaining? (We've all been there!) What did the grumbling and complaining produce?

Do you know you shine like a star when you're following in Christ's footsteps? Who are some of the stars in your life? In other words, who is an inspiration to you as Allison was an inspiration to me?

While writing out Philippians 2:12-16, think about the people you've known who have truly delighted in serving behind the scenes. Let them serve as real-life examples of what it means to walk in Christ's footsteps.

Prayer: Thank You, Lord, for being the greatest example of what it means to live as a humble servant. Help me to serve in hidden ways with a glad and sincere heart. Help me to be the kind of person who holds pom-poms for someone else, cheering and supporting the success of others. Amen.

Day 12

Offering with Gladness

Open my eyes so that I may contemplate wonderful things from Your instruction.

PSALM 119:18

I hear the technician speak into the microphone, "Exhale slowly. Now hold it. Hold it. Okay. Go ahead and exhale all the way." I hear more beeps as the magnetic resonance imager takes pictures of my husband's insides. I'm not allowed to be in the room with him, so I have to sit around the corner from the technician. Through a large pane of glass, I can see Jeff's sock feet sticking out of the giant tube he's lying in.

"Okay. Inhale. Hold it. Now exhale. Hold it. A little longer. Now breathe out again."

I realize I'm following the technician's instructions to my husband. I'm holding my breath, even though I'm not the one having pictures taken of my liver and pancreas. My husband's symptoms scare us both beyond words. Something's not right, and we're praying like there's no tomorrow that the MRI rules out pancreatic cancer. Because a diagnosis like that would likely mean few tomorrows are left.

At night we lie in silence, still holding our breath. All we can do is hold each other and try not to cry. Inside my heart I'm begging God for mercy. But we have to wait a couple of days for the results, so we agree to go back to work and try to resume some normalcy even though a dark cloud overshadows us.

The next morning, I sit at my desk in my classroom, thankful my first period is a prep. I can be alone for another hour. But I'm angry. Why would God allow this? This was the very reason we almost didn't get married. Jeff's dad died when he was 10. Then his mom died when he was 24. He spent the rest of his twenties raising his youngest sister. The thought of dying young, like both of his parents, and leaving a family behind was too much to risk. So Jeff remained a bachelor for a long time. Until he met me.

For Jeff, getting married and having children was a huge leap of faith, much more so than for the average person. And now? Our son, Parker, is 10 years old, the same age Jeff was when his dad died. The coincidence of the timing is too much, and I'm growing angrier by the minute that God might allow our worst fears to come true. I can't imagine Jeff having to say good-bye to his kids, knowing exactly what they would go through—because he had already been through it himself.

"God, that's just cruel."

Then I hear God speak to my heart, not with an audible voice, but with words I know I could never come up with on my own: *How did Jeff turn out?*

Jeff endured horrific loss, but by God's grace, he grew into the most caring, responsible husband and father anyone could ask for.

"God, that's not fair. I know Jeff turned out great. And, yeah, I suppose You're trying to tell me to trust that our kids would turn out fine too. But I don't want to go down that road. I don't want to trust You with my kids."

My own words reveal my fear. I don't want to trust God to take care of our kids. I want Jeff and me to take care of our kids. No one else.

"Okay, God, I get it. I want to trust You to take care of our kids. But I'm afraid of the process. I'm afraid that I'll still become so angry with You that I won't just lose Jeff, I'll lose You too. And that scares me more than anything." And there was my deepest fear of all: becoming so angry with God that I'd turn my back on Him.

"God, I'm still begging You for mercy on Jeff and our kids and me. But if the worst happens, please hold on to me even if I'm tempted to let go of You. I know I wouldn't survive without You."

My desk in my classroom becomes an altar as I surrender everything to God in the face of our worst "even if" fear.

Read Numbers 15:1-12 and Philippians 2:17-18

Paul says, "even if I am poured out as a drink offering on the sacrifice and service of your faith, I am glad and rejoice with all of you" (2:17). Knowing he might die a martyr's death, Paul likens the spilling of his own blood to the Old Testament pouring of a drink offering. And we can see in the book of Numbers those "drink offerings" weren't consumed. They were poured out as part of a sacrifice. The sacrifices in the Old Testament foreshadowed the ultimate sacrifice that would come—Jesus, the Lamb of God (see John 1:29)—who would lay down His life on the cross for all of us. Just as the Old Testament drink offerings point to Jesus, Paul considers his possible martyrdom as a "drink offering" that would point others to Jesus. And Paul sees such an offering as a source of deep gladness.

In Day 9 we talked about "sacrificing for the sake of others" as one of the steps toward a life of deeper joy. Paul now takes this step further by saying "even if." Even if he's called to make the ultimate sacrifice and give his life for Christ, he sees such an offering as a source of deep gladness.

As Jeff and I waited for the results of his MRI along with the results of a dozen other tests, we did our best, individually and together, to embrace our "even if." I can't say we experienced a joyful gladness over the prospect, but I can say we both experienced a peace in His presence. This is one of the hardest steps toward a life of deeper joy: being at peace with whatever direction life takes. Even if.

> God won't ever leave us, even when we're tempted to leave Him.
>
> #WordWriters

Thankfully, the results came back with a better-than-most prognosis. Jeff's liver was reacting adversely, but with time, he'd be okay. I know the results don't always come back with good news for everyone. And if there's ever a "next time" for us, the results might not come back with good news for us either. But I do know this: God won't ever leave us, even when we're tempted to leave Him.

Diving Deeper

In verses 17 and 18, how many times do the words *glad* and *rejoice* appear? (If you're using a New Living Translation, how many times do the words *joy* and *rejoice* appear?)

In Numbers 15, what did the drink offering consist of? (See verses 5, 7, and 10.)

Wine is mostly associated with times of great joy, such as wedding celebrations. So the pouring out of wine is a symbolic way of saying, "the greater the sacrifice, the greater the joy."* When have you experienced a deep joy in tandem with a great sacrifice?

When have you surrendered your worst fear to God? What did God teach you during this time?

---

* John Phillips, *Exploring Ephesians and Philippians: An Expository Commentary* (Grand Rapids, MI: Kregel Publications, 1993), 102.

While writing out Philippians 2:17-18, ask God to help you be at peace with whatever direction life takes.

Prayer: Thank You, Lord, for holding on to me, even when I'm tempted to let go of You. Forgive me when I let my fear pull me from You. Help me to surrender my every fear to You. Help me to trust You with everything—and everyone—in my life. I love You, and I want my life to show it, in everything I do. Amen.

Brimming with Kindness

Open my eyes so that I may contemplate wonderful things from Your instruction.

PSALM 119:18

I stare at the job application, wondering what I'm supposed to put in the next blank. To teach at a Christian school, I need to write the name of a spiritual mentor. You know, like a spiritual reference. But the word *mentor* sounds so formal. And I've never had a mentor. Not formally anyway. But I can think of a lot of women who have influenced me over the years. Women who have taught me by their example.

The first woman I can distinctly remember influencing me was my youth pastor's wife, Kandee. As a senior in high school, I loved going to youth group. Our new youth pastor was as rambunctious and energetic as his wife was soft-spoken and mild-mannered. Together, they made a great team. Soon after coming to our church, they bought their first home. With new paint and carpet, they were excited about fixing up their own place. Kandee had a blast picking out the colors. But they made the classic decision I've since learned many young couples make: Against all advice, they chose to have nearly white carpet installed.

Once my youth pastor and his wife were settled into their new home, they invited the youth group over for a party. I enjoyed hanging out in the kitchen, helping Kandee serve the food and drinks, but after a while, I filled my plate with some chips and moseyed into the living room. I held my plate on my lap and placed my cup of grape soda safely beneath my chair. Twenty minutes later, I tried to climb over the teenagers filling every square inch of the house, and I accidentally knocked over my cup.

I'm not sure why I feel the need, 25 years later, to reiterate that this was an *accident*. Of course it was an accident! But what difference does it make when a puddle the size of a basketball bore the indelible mark of my disgrace in a sparkling shade of permanent plum?

Desperate, and near frantic, I worked feverishly to sop up my mess while begging God not to let it stain. God did not answer my prayer. That's when Kandee came to see what all the gasps were about. My face was about as red as the white carpet was purple. I was in tears.

To assuage my fears, Kandee put her hand on my shoulder and assured me it wasn't a big deal. Naturally, I didn't believe her. This was their first new home! It was brand-new carpet! And I had ruined it.

"Please," she said, "don't give it another thought. I wasn't planning on taking that carpet with me to heaven anyway."

I could tell, much to my own surprise, she wasn't acting. She was calm. Unnaturally calm. Or perhaps, supernaturally calm.

Today, I can't remember a single sermon the youth pastor ever preached, although I know I listened intently at the time. But I will always remember the grace his wife showed me when I was so undeserving. Her warmth and sincerity gave new meaning to Job's words, "Naked I came from my mother's womb, and naked I will leave this life" (Job 1:21). She showed me grace while also modeling the importance of not clinging to the material things of this world. Nowadays, whenever I have a guest in my home and something happens to break or become stained, it's a privilege for me to say, "Oh, don't worry about that. I wasn't planning on taking it with me to heaven anyway." My youth pastor's wife will forever be one of my "hidden heroes."

Read Philippians 2:19-24

In chapter 2, Paul continues his discussion of examples to follow. He starts with the greatest example: Jesus (2:5-11). Then he uses himself as an example in the way he's okay with being "poured out as a drink offering" for the sake of others (2:17). Now he's talking about Timothy, who is like a son to him. Paul says Timothy genuinely cares about their interests, and he's a man of proven character. So Paul hopes to send Timothy to the believers in Philippi soon, to be an encouragement to them.

At first glance, I'll admit I'm tempted to envy the kind of mentor relationship Timothy had with Paul. I would love to have a mentor like that! But long before Paul came along, Timothy's faith was already growing strong because Timothy had a grandma and a mom who loved Jesus with everything they had. Grandma Lois and Mama Eunice taught young Timothy everything they knew about the Scriptures (see 2 Timothy 1:5). They cultivated the soil of Timothy's soul, so by the time Paul came into Timothy's life, the young man was eager and ready to learn all he could from the missionary apostle.

> Mentoring another person is a way of investing in God's kingdom.
>
> #WordWriters

Timothy's life is an example of the kind of impact a grandma and a mom can make for future generations. And we're invited to follow in their footsteps, not only with our own children, but also with other women who yearn to have someone speak into their lives. We can be like my youth pastor's wife, who invested in me by simply spending time with me and showing me what grace and kindness look like. Mentoring another person is one of the greatest ways we can invest in God's kingdom. This is the next step toward a life of deeper joy: investing in the life of another person.

Diving Deeper

Why is Paul so confident in Timothy?

What does Paul mean in verse 24 when he says, "I am convinced in the Lord that I myself will also come quickly"?

Have you ever had a mentor? Who are some of the women who have influenced you to be more like Christ?

Are you mentoring someone now? No matter our age, we can always invest in someone! Who can you begin investing in today?

As you write out Philippians 2:19-24, ask God to show you who you can begin investing in. If you're already mentoring someone, ask God to show you a specific way you can encourage your mentee today.

Prayer: Thank You, Lord, for the women You have brought into my life over the years. Each one has taught me something of Your character. Help me to become the kind of woman who invests in others. Help me to be like Grandma Lois and Mama Eunice to the younger women in my church and in my community. Help me to show them who You are. Amen.

Honoring with Reverence

Open my eyes so that I may contemplate wonderful things from Your instruction.

PSALM 119:18

When our daughter Brynn was four years old, she reacted in wonder when we explained that *her* grandma was *my* mom. We smiled as we watched her put the family pieces together. Then one day she asked, "Daddy, where are your mom and dad?"

"Well, they're not here, honey. They passed away a long time ago."

As I shared in a previous story, my husband lost his parents fairly early in life, and my parents live hundreds of miles away. So as far as regular, everyday life goes, it's just our little family, doing life, mostly without grandparents around for our kids. But one silver-haired couple at church has been a godsend to us. On Sunday mornings, Bob and Diana have hugged our kids as they walk to Sunday school. They've invited us over for dinner, pulling up an extra chair to the table. They've even remembered our kids' birthdays, stopping by our house with presents for the kids.

Bob and Diana have been sort of like our kids' "local grandparents." Words can't express how much they mean to us. Sometimes Jeff and I will talk late into the night about the kind of couple we want to be. We agree; we want to be like Bob and Diana. We want to be the kind of people who widen the circle of our family.

One Saturday morning, Bob and Diana invited us over for breakfast. They made blueberry pancakes, scrambled eggs, and crispy bacon. They even started a fire in the fireplace to honor us as their guests. You would think little kids would moan at the prospect of going to the home of a retired couple. But when we told our kids we were going to Bob and Diana's, they whooped and hollered.

They couldn't wait. Bob is a retired woodshop teacher, and he's built a tree house with a zip line in his backyard. The kids have been playing in that tree house for years, creating some of the sweetest childhood memories.

Read Philippians 2:25-30

Paul finishes chapter 2 with one final example of a genuine follower of Christ, Epaphroditus, who came from Philippi to bring Paul a financial gift from the church. Paul heralds Epaphroditus, a faithful friend who nearly died from illness while traveling to visit him in Rome, and he gives explicit instructions in his letter for the church in Philippi to honor Epaphroditus when he returns. Paul says to "hold men like him in honor" (2:29).

Men and women are serving in our churches today whom we should honor as well. This is the next step toward a life of deeper joy: honoring men and women who serve. They may hold a position in the church with a title, or they may not. It could be someone like Diana, who walks through every Sunday school classroom before church, praying for each child who will be in that classroom later in the morning. Or it could be someone like Bob, who shows up on a Tuesday morning with a tool belt around his waist, ready to fix a leaky water heater or unplug a plugged toilet. Bob and Diana are hidden heroes. They've touched many lives beyond my own family.

> Hidden heroes impact God's kingdom one heart at a time.
>
> #WordWriters

Hidden heroes are the biggest difference makers of all, because they impact the kingdom one heart at a time. You likely have hidden heroes in your church too. Perhaps you're one of them. If not, you can be, starting today. All it takes is a heart willing to look to the interests of others.

Diving Deeper

Why does Paul feel it's necessary to send Epaphroditus to Philippi right away?

What happened to Epaphroditus while he was in Rome with Paul?

Are you like Timothy, in that you had a godly grandmother, mother, or both, who taught you the Scriptures? Or have you had a Bob and Diana in your life, who in some ways "filled the gap" where a grandparent or parent might have been?

Who are the hidden heroes in your life? How can you honor them today?

Write out Philippians 2:25-30 and ask God to show you a way you can honor the hidden heroes in your life.

Prayer: Thank You, Lord, for the men and women who serve in so many ways—even in ways we might not see. Show me how I can honor them with due reverence. Teach me, Lord, to become more like these humble servants, who don't need titles or accolades. Help me to grow in humility and in service. Amen.

A Call to See Beyond
~ our qualifications ~

After giving us several examples to follow, Paul goes on to explain that we need to set aside the earthly things we think are important. But before Paul continues, he pauses at the midpoint in his letter to say, "Rejoice in the Lord" (3:1). Perhaps we could follow his example and simply pause, wherever we are in our day, to rejoice in the Lord. Tell Him how good He is, and tell Him how much we love Him.

Why Repetition Matters

Open my eyes so that I may contemplate wonderful things from Your instruction.

PSALM 119:18

In 2009, a group of us circled a table at church, ready for Bible study and prayer. It was my favorite time of the week—being with women, studying God's Word. We talked about Esther—how God orchestrated events for her to save her people (Esther 4:14). We talked about Deborah—how God chose her to lead Israel (Judges 4–5). We talked about Priscilla—how God led her and her husband to train Apollos in the truth of Scripture (Acts 18:24-28). God used these women and so many more in valiant ways in His kingdom.

Our Bible study leader, Carolyn, looked at each of us around the table and asked, "How does God want to use you in His kingdom? What is He calling you to do?"

I held back, not wanting to answer the question. I let the other women talk first. I had been thinking of something for a while, but it seemed so silly I didn't want to tell anyone about it. A friend of mine had recently moved away, and she had started a blog to share stories and pictures of their new life in another state. At the time I didn't know anything about blogs, but the more I looked into it, the more the idea of a blog intrigued me. Except I had a different direction in mind. I imagined a blog where I might write devotions based on Scripture. I didn't know if other blogs did that sort of thing. The only blogs I knew of were blogs about motherhood.

Carolyn and the other women around the table looked at me. It was my turn. So I mumbled something about writing devotions and a blog, certain that everyone would give me a blank stare. But Carolyn's response took me by surprise. "I have a blog," she said, "and I join a group of women every Tuesday to write a devotion. We write our thoughts on the same quote. Sometimes it's a passage from the Bible. Other times it's a passage from a Christian book. It's really fun. You should join us!"

So I did. And I loved it. Writing devotions for women has brought me a joy I didn't know possible.

Read Philippians 3:1-3

I love how Paul begins this section of Scripture. He says it's no trouble at all for him to write the same things. Paul isn't writing stuff they've never heard of. His letter to the Philippians isn't revealing new truths. His letter is a reiteration of truths they already know. His letter is simply an encouragement to keep God's truth fresh on their hearts.

For the longest time, this was my biggest hang-up when it came to writing. Solomon said in Ecclesiastes, "There's nothing new under the sun" (1:9). So why would anyone want to read something I wrote? Hasn't everything already been said? It has. But repetition isn't a bad thing. God uses voices in every generation to encourage others. And that's what I want to do with my words: encourage women to draw closer to God through studying and writing His Word.

Repetition has always been a useful learning tool. Whether we're learning the multiplication table or the periodic table, we learn through the repetition of facts and key ideas. The same is true in the Bible. Whenever we see the same idea repeated in Scripture, that's our first clue. Repetition in the Bible is a cue to slow down and review. This is why Paul says to the Philippians, "To write to you again about this is no trouble for me and is a protection for you" (3:1). This is Paul's way of waving a big sign that says, *Okay. We're about to review something we've talked about before, but it's super important, so we need to go over it again.* Paul then warns the believers not to become distracted by

> Repetition in the Bible is a cue to slow down and review.
>
> #WordWriters

those who try to add to God's grace. Our salvation is by faith in Jesus Christ alone. Not faith plus good works. Not faith plus the law of Moses. Not faith plus circumcision.

You would think everyone would tire of Paul repeating himself so much on this point. But it's foundational to everything Paul preaches and everything we believe. We cannot work our way to heaven, so why would we ever boast about our works at all? When we've surrendered our lives to Christ, we recognize this truth: Apart from God, we can do nothing. But with God, we can accomplish more than we ever thought possible. This is the next step in cultivating a life of deeper joy: stepping into the calling God has placed on our lives.

What is the first command Paul gives in chapter 3?

Why is Paul so adamant about "watching out" for those "mutilators of the flesh"?

How does God want to use you in His kingdom? What is He calling you to do?

Let's write Philippians 3:1-3 today, thanking God for the specific calling He has placed on each of our lives.

Prayer: Thank You, Lord, for calling me to a specific task. Help me to move forward in the calling You have placed on my life. Help me to reach out to other women too, so we can be an encouragement to one another. I pray that all I say and do will bring glory to You. Amen.

What Really Counts

Open my eyes so that I may contemplate wonderful things from Your instruction.

PSALM 119:18

I enjoy all kinds of writing. Short stories. Essays. Letters. Even research papers. But one of my favorite things to write is a letter of recommendation, because it's a special way to honor someone I believe has not only worked hard in my classroom, but has also demonstrated great character. When I write a recommendation, I quickly cover the basics: good grades and other academic achievements. But that's what everyone's letter will say, so I like to move beyond the basics and talk about the things you won't find on a résumé. A typical résumé is a list of earned degrees and previous job titles. It's a highlight reel of a professional career. But a résumé is only one-dimensional.

Résumés don't tell you what students do when they finish their work. Do they find something else to work on? Do they help a neighbor? Or do they put their head on their desk and take a nap instead? Résumés don't tell you how students respond to a poor score. Do they argue the answer key is wrong? Do they question the validity of the test? Or do they ask for extra help to better understand the nature of where they missed the mark?

A résumé can boast of certain achievements, but it cannot convey the character of a person. And in my estimation, that's what really counts. In today's reading, Paul writes his résumé. By Hebrew standards, it's a top-notch résumé, too, and for a long time, Paul was convinced his résumé meant he was superior to most people.

Read Philippians 3:4-7

Paul explains that none of the qualifications on his résumé mean anything to him anymore. He says everything he once put so much confidence in is actually garbage! His so-called qualifications have zero worth. All that matters to him now is knowing Christ and having His character.

Character counts. God has given each of us a calling, but our character must match our calling. What we do when no one is looking counts. What we do when we're finished with our work counts. What we do when we're under pressure counts.

This is the next step toward a life of deeper joy: building a life of great character. This is far more important than building an impressive résumé.

Diving Deeper

Why does Paul encourage the Philippians not to put their confidence in the flesh? What does he mean by this?

Who does Paul say we should put our confidence in?

Why does Paul say he considers everything a loss because of Christ?

When have you put your confidence in your own qualifications or previous accomplishments? Is Paul saying we should never be confident at all?

As you write Philippians 3:4-7 today, ask God to show you how you can build your character, in ways both large and small, each and every day.

Prayer: Thank You, Lord, for imparting Your righteousness to Your children. Forgive me when I'm tempted to boast in my own accomplishments. Help me to build a life of great character. May my life be a testament to all that You have done in me. Amen.

Day 17

Where Hope Is Found

Open my eyes so that I may contemplate wonderful things from Your instruction.

PSALM 119:18

We all experience suffering in this life—some more than others. But few people experience anything as devastating as losing their entire family. I know only one person who lost her entire family. My Grandma Lucy enjoyed being a wife and a mom throughout her twenties. But when her son was eleven years old, he drowned while swimming in the Columbia River. Then a short while later, her husband was killed in a railroad accident. My grandma's entire family was taken from her—first her only child, then her husband.

Throughout her thirties, during the Great Depression, my grandma worked cleaning houses. Then she met my grandpa when she was nearly forty years old. After they married, she gave birth to my dad, and a few years later, to a little girl. At this point, there should be a "happily ever after." But when my grandma's daughter was three years old, she died of leukemia. This has never made any sense to me. Hadn't my grandma suffered enough?

Grandma Lucy endured more loss and suffering than most people will experience in a lifetime, but all I can remember is an elderly woman who continued to praise God to the very end of her 94 years of life. In today's reading, Paul says his only goal is to know Christ and "the power of His resurrection and the fellowship of His sufferings" (3:10). Whenever I read these words, I'll be honest, I think they sound dreary. Why would anyone voluntarily sign up to suffer? That's plain morbid. So what is Paul talking about here? Let's read.

Read Philippians 3:8-11

When Paul says he wants to know Christ and the fellowship of His suffer-ings, he's saying he wants Christ more than anything this world has to offer. He wants Christ more than he wants the respect of his peers. He wants Christ more than he wants a reputable career. He wants Christ more than anything, even if it means suffering for Christ's sake.

I don't know why God allowed my grandma to suffer so much loss. It seems to me she experienced more than her "fair share." But when I think this way, what I'm really saying is I think there is x amount of suffering to go around, and Someone ought to parcel it out more evenly. But that's not how suffering works. And that's not how God works. Suffering is the inevitable result of sin in the world.

> Waiting on God to make all things right again is where our hope is found.
>
> #WordWriters

Most people respond to severe suffering in one of two ways: Either they enter into the natural griev-ing process and cling to God through it all, or they resist the grieving process and resent God through it all. Somehow my grandma clung to God, knowing one day she'd be with her loved ones again. Today I know exactly where she is. She's in His presence, along with everyone she once lost. This is one of the hard-est steps of living a life of deeper joy: waiting on God until He makes all things right again. But this is where hope is found—in Christ alone.

Diving Deeper

When Paul says in verse 8 he has "suffered the loss of all things," what is he refer-ring to? (Look back at Philippians 3:4-6.)

Have you known someone who experienced more than their "fair share" of suffering? How did this person respond to such suffering?

In the twenty-first century, what does it look like to share in the fellowship of Christ's suffering? In what ways have you shared in the fellowship of Christ's suffering?

While writing out Philippians 3:8-11, ask God to make His presence known. We need His grace to see us through whatever life brings.

Prayer: Thank You, Lord, for promising to be with me no matter what comes my way. Forgive me when I'm tempted to compare my suffering with others. Soften my heart and help me to learn what it means to suffer for Your name. When I'm hurting, help me to look to You to get me through. Because in You, I have real hope. Amen.

A Call to See Beyond
~ our disqualifications ~

Paul turns his discussion to the past—specifically, to *our* past. He calls us to see beyond our past, to refuse to let it blind us from the future we have in Christ. Past sin? It's gone. Because of the cross, we're new creations. Former failures do not disqualify us from the future goals that God has purposed for us.

Forgetting What Is Behind

Open my eyes so that I may contemplate wonderful things from Your instruction.

PSALM 119:18

When I heard the shot fire, I ran as fast as possible. After the first turn in the lane, I could tell I was ahead of the pack. Way ahead. This race would be a cinch. For all the headache of being taller than most boys in the seventh grade, this was the one place where I appreciated my long legs.

Curiosity got the better of me, though, and I looked back to see what kind of margin I had. A smile crossed my face as I determined this race to be an easy win. I kept running, but I was interested to see how things were going behind me. So I stole another backward glimpse. This time, a girl seemed a little closer. I pushed harder. Then once more I glanced over my shoulder. She was closing in. By the time we reached the finish line, she had edged me out of the blue ribbon.

Panting and hunched over, I heard my coach coming toward me and I'll never forget his words. "Why did you look back? You could have won if you hadn't looked back! Looking back always slows a runner down!"

I couldn't believe it. My coach knew the secret to finishing first and he waited till now to tell me?

Looking back always slows a runner down.

I've never forgotten this lesson. Sometimes it's important, necessary even, to consider events of the past, to reflect and learn from them. But there comes a time when we need to stop dwelling on the past. In today's reading, Paul admonishes us to forget what is behind and focus on what is ahead.

Read Philippians 3:12-16

In more than one place, Scripture refers to our journey through life as a race. Not necessarily a sprint, but a marathon because the call to follow Jesus is daily and forever. Our lane is marked out for us too. God has a purpose for each of our lives, a distinct calling for each of us to fulfill. But when we're focused on how other people are doing in their lanes, we get sidetracked from our own race and it slows us down. When we run the "race marked out for us" (Hebrews 12:1 NIV), our lives become a testament for His glory. This is another step toward a life of deeper joy: leaving our past in the past by forgetting what is behind and focusing on what is ahead.

> Former failures do not disqualify us from the future goals that God has purposed for us.
>
> #WordWriters

All too often, though, our regrets from the past overshadow our joy in the present. But this isn't what God wants for us. When we ask God to forgive us, He wipes the slate clean. We're forgiven. Totally and completely. Psalm 103:12 says, "As far as the east is from the west, so far has He removed our transgressions from us." This doesn't mean God cannot remember our past; it means He no longer holds our past against us. God has set us free from our past! When we refuse to let go of the past, we're actually refusing to accept the fullness of God's grace. Let's humble ourselves instead, and ask God to give us the grace and power we need to move on.

Diving Deeper

Why does Paul emphasize the fact that he hasn't yet "arrived" at a place of perfection? Why is it important to remember that we're all a work in progress?

How can our focus on the past inhibit us from running the race God has for us?

What are some ways you can stay focused on running the race marked out for you?

Let's write out Philippians 3:12-16 with a renewed passion for the race before us!

Prayer: Thank You, Lord, for choosing this particular time and place in history for me to run my race. Help me to trust You with my whole being. I know You've called me to live for Your glory. Give me the grace I need to run this one race well. Amen.

Focusing on What Lies Ahead

Open my eyes so that I may contemplate wonderful things from Your instruction.

PSALM 119:18

My Grandma Lucy was the sweetest grandma you could ever imagine. She was as sweet as her sweet tooth, and I loved going to her place. Grandma always greeted me with a fresh stash of something yummy. And by "fresh," I mean "just out of the wrapper." Grandma liked to tuck a few Snickers bars in the space next to the forks and spoons, and she never ran out of orange sherbet ice cream. She was 67 years old when I was born, so by the time I was old enough to ride my bike over to her house, she was well into her seventies.

I visited Grandma every day, not because of the candy bars, but because I enjoyed her company. She taught me how to play pinochle and Chinese checkers, and whenever I had an art project at school, she'd take me to the "dime store" for art supplies. Her favorite book besides the Bible was an almanac. She'd buy a new edition every year, and she'd read it to me whenever she happened upon something interesting.

As a high school student, I'd walk to her apartment after school and spend several hours there before going to my own house, just a few blocks away. It's safe to say my best friend in high school was a woman in her eighties. And as I mentioned earlier in this study, she lived to be 94. Grandma's memory held up, too, until the last couple years of her life. But the last time I visited her, she didn't remember me.

After Grandma's funeral, my brother and I sat next to her grave, remembering our favorite stories about her. My brother, Kendall, has been paralyzed since he was 19, and he sat in his wheelchair while I sat on the grass. Kendall said the last time he visited Grandma, she couldn't remember him either. He said he knew it would probably be the last time he'd see her alive, so before he left he took her hand and said, "Grandma, the next time you see me, you're going to be able to remember me, and I'm going to be able to walk up to you and give you a hug."

Isn't this what we're all longing for? To be made whole again?

Read Philippians 3:17-21

Since joy is the predominant theme in Paul's letter, I can't think of a better reason to celebrate than knowing one day our broken bodies, minds, and hearts will be made new! My grandma is with Jesus now. Her mind is restored. And when my brother sees Jesus, he'll step out of that wheelchair and dance his way into eternity. Paul says so in Philippians: "Our citizenship is in heaven, from which we also eagerly wait for a Savior, the Lord Jesus Christ. He will transform the body of our humble condition into the likeness of His glorious body" (3:20-21). He repeats this same truth in his letter to the Corinthians too: "Indeed, we groan in this body, desiring to put on our dwelling from heaven" (2 Corinthians 5:2). The disciple John also said as much in his letter: "Dear friends, we are God's children now, and what we will be has not yet been revealed. We know that when He appears, we will be like Him" (1 John 3:2). This is the best reason of all to live with a deeper joy now: knowing that one day we'll be made whole.

> We can live with deeper joy, knowing that one day we'll be made whole.
>
> #WordWriters

Diving Deeper

Paul invites us to imitate not only him, but those who live in a way that pleases God. Who in your life do you want to imitate?

Where is your true citizenship?

When the day finally comes when you see Jesus face-to-face, what are you most looking forward to?

While writing Philippians 3:17-21, let's thank Him that our imperfect bodies here on earth will one day be exchanged for a new body—whole and well—when we see Jesus. What a day that will be!

Prayer: Thank You, Lord, for the promise we have of being made whole. Help me when I struggle to get through the day, wondering why so much heartache and brokenness pervades this earthly existence. I know You created us to be whole. And the work of the cross promises that we'll be whole again soon. In You I rejoice that one day all things will be made new! Amen!

A Call to See Beyond
~the worries of this world~

Paul is relentless in his desire for us to live beyond the worries of this world. And he takes no prisoners. He wants to see God's people set free! From conflict. From worry. From anything that bars us from experiencing the fullness that is ours in Christ Jesus. So get ready. Because Paul is about to get personal. In the nicest kind of way.

When Conflict Arises

Open my eyes so that I may contemplate wonderful things from Your instruction.

PSALM 119:18

The invitation I'd been waiting for finally came! I was attending a new church and had looked into the various ways I could get involved. Since it was a smaller church, there wasn't a formal small group ministry. They said they wanted small groups to happen organically. Well, there was one particular group of young women I wanted to befriend. Funny enough, we'd all had a baby boy within the previous year, and I was longing for companionship with other moms. I soon learned these women were all in the same small group together. But when I asked how I could join them, I was informed it was a closed group. They weren't accepting new members.

My heart sank. Part of me wanted to leave the church and try somewhere else. But I didn't want to be a "church hopper," so I prayed and asked God to show me where I should get plugged in. That's when the invitation came! A new small group was forming with several of the women who had recently joined the church. Would I like to join? You bet!

Eight of us started meeting every Monday night. We'd read a passage of Scripture, talk about it, and pray. Then we'd spend the rest of the evening chatting, getting to know one another. We planned a weekend getaway for just the eight of us too. Our new group was growing close, and I was grateful to be a part. I had noticed that two of the women became immediate best friends, and the other five women seemed to be spending time together during the week. I hadn't yet developed a close relationship with any one person, but I was content to be among the group.

One Monday night we gathered like normal, but then one woman accused another woman of being unkind. It quickly became clear that something had been brewing for some time, and the others all seemed to know about it. Our group split, with the five women against the two. Sadly, our group never recovered. The five women continued to talk about their grievances with other people in the church; they even went before the elder board to complain about the two women. To be honest, I didn't think the original offense warranted such vehemence. The two women had apologized for the perceived hurts they had apparently caused, but the five women wouldn't relent until the other two eventually left the church.

I wish I could say this sort of thing rarely happens in church settings, but I'm afraid rifts such as this one are all too common. In today's reading, we see a similar conflict between women in Philippi.

Read Philippians 4:1-5

Paul urges the Philippians to help two women, Euodia and Syntyche, heal a fractured relationship. He pleads with them to "agree in the Lord." He remembers the way they had once worked together, side by side, for the gospel. Paul goes on to say their names are written in the book of life. These women are believers, yet for whatever reason they're at odds with each other. And we know their conflict led to negative ramifications for the whole church because everyone knew about it. Even Paul heard about it in Rome!

> Whenever conflict is present, we need to seek the grace of God's presence.
>
> #WordWriters

We can learn several things from the situation between Euodia and Syntyche. One, they didn't keep the matter between themselves. They talked about their situation to other folks, and the other folks ended up taking sides. Now the problem is even bigger. Unity in the church is at stake. Two, we see that Paul chooses not to divulge any details. The details aren't important. And Paul isn't going to spread the infection any further. Three, Paul appeals to the one thing they all have in common: the Lord. "Rejoice in the Lord always," he says. "I will say it again: Rejoice!" (4:4). He encourages them to fix their gaze heavenward. Whenever conflict is present, we need the grace of His presence.

When we're experiencing a fissure in a relationship, we want to prayerfully and humbly reconcile with the person directly involved. If that doesn't work, we can ask someone from leadership to help us mediate our differences (see Matthew 18:15-17). What we don't want to do is share "our side of things" with whoever will listen. That only furthers ill will. Paul implores the Philippians to let their "graciousness be known to everyone" (4:5). Oh that we would be a grace-filled people. This is such an important step toward a life of deeper joy: Handling conflict with humility, grace, and wisdom.

Diving Deeper

What does Paul ask of the church in Philippi in regard to Euodia and Syntyche?

When have you experienced or observed a relational conflict in the church handled with the utmost grace and care? What did you learn from the situation?

Since we live in a fallen world and relational conflict is inevitable, in what ways are you committed to handling potential conflict with humility, grace, and wisdom?

With each word of Philippians 4:1-5 you write, ask God to help you become an instrument of peace in your relationships and your church.

Prayer: Thank You, Lord, for providing clear instructions in Your Word for how Your children are to handle conflict. Help me to be a person who is quick to listen, slow to speak, and slow to become angry. As far as it depends on me, help me to be at peace with everyone. Amen.

Day 21

When Worry Takes Over

Open my eyes so that I may contemplate wonderful things from Your instruction.

PSALM 119:18

I remember the first time I attended a Bible study by Beth Moore. The study was called *Believing God* and part of the homework suggested a weekly memory verse. I felt convicted because I used to be diligent about memorizing Scripture, but somehow I'd fallen out of practice. As the weeks wore on, I hung in there pretty well, but I was a graduate student at the time, preparing to take my comprehensive exams, which would last a grueling nine hours. I also had three young children at the time.

On the last day of the Bible study, the women who had memorized all ten Bible verses were asked to stand up and share the verses with everyone in the room. Nobody stood up. Again, I felt guilty. I really wanted to memorize all ten. I had made it to nine, but then quit. Instead, I devoted every waking minute to memorizing passages by Plato and Aristotle, the key sections I would need to recall when taking my exams.

Then Marci, a woman in her sixties, stood up. Slowly, she began to recite each verse. Word by word. Phrase by phrase. With long pauses between each one. The rest of us in the room could only watch silently, agonizing with her as she tried to remember each line. If someone offered to give her the starting word of the next phrase, she would hold up her hand and shake her head. Marci wanted to do this. All of it. By herself.

She continued. Ever so slowly. Word by word. Phrase by phrase.

We sat there holding our breath. Would she make it? Another long pause. Then, about the time we thought it was over and she'd give up, she'd come through with the next phrase. We'd all breathe again. Finally, ten minutes later,

Marci recited the last memory verse. She did it! Without any help from anyone. The room exploded in applause.

When our cheering quieted down, Marci shared with us how her mother suffered from Alzheimer's. She had witnessed this terrible disease steal her mother's memory, so she wanted to memorize these verses to prove to herself that she could still remember. Tears flowed. Both hers and ours. She still had her memory. And we rejoiced with her.

Marci's commitment to finish inspired me. Somewhere along the way, I had gotten bogged down with worry; I had gotten too busy. It's funny how *worry* and *busy* go together. I worried about my graduate courses. I worried about what I'd fix for dinner. I worried about how we'd pay for our oldest daughter's braces. I worried about the decades-old air conditioner that was sure to quit on us when it was 100 degrees outside. I worried about everything. And while I worried, I failed to meditate on God's Word. It's funny how *worry* and *busy* and *failure to meditate on God's Word* go together.

Read Philippians 4:6-9

In today's reading, Paul gets direct. He doesn't tiptoe around the issue. He says it straight: "Don't worry about anything" (4:6). Um, okay, but isn't that easier said than done? Worry can grow in our minds the way weeds can grow in a garden. We must be diligent to uproot worry before it leads us down a trail of negative thought patterns. Our actions begin with our thoughts, which is why it's so important that we "take our thoughts captive" and examine them under the light of God's truth (see 2 Corinthians 10:5). This is an essential step toward a life of deeper joy: dwelling only on things that are true and good and beautiful.

> Uproot worry before it grows like weeds. Dwell on pure thoughts to plant positive seeds.
>
> #WordWriters

------------------------------ *Diving Deeper* ------------------------------

What is Paul's antidote to worry?

If we dwell on Him and all that is good, with what does God promise to guard our hearts?

Do you ever find yourself dwelling on the negative, worrying about things that haven't even happened yet? How can you begin to combat worry?

As you write out Philippians 4:6-9, say it out loud as another way of reminding your heart that it needs to dwell on things that are true, honorable, just, pure, lovely, commendable, excellent, and praiseworthy!

Prayer: Thank You, Lord, for providing a way to combat worry and other negative thoughts that enter my mind. Help me when I'm tempted to dwell on the negative. Help me to uproot these thoughts and take them captive! Your Word is alive and active, and the more I internalize Your Word, the more Your truth permeates my heart and mind. Amen.

A Call to See Beyond
~ our discontent ~

A common thread ties joy with peace and contentment. I can't even imagine one without the other. How could joy be possible without peace? How could peace be possible without contentment? Whenever I'm wrestling with feelings of discontent, I have neither peace nor joy. It's no wonder the enemy works so hard to stir up seeds of discontent within our souls. When we're focused on what we lack—on what we still want—we forget how much we already have, and we forfeit our own joy.

The Secret of Contentment

Open my eyes so that I may contemplate wonderful things from Your instruction.

PSALM 119:18

When I was 19, I moved into my first apartment. Even though it was furnished with a mismatched collection of hand-me-down furniture, it was mine and I loved it. I normally went to work every day, but since my car needed a repair, I was home one afternoon waiting for the tow truck to arrive. When I heard a loud knock on my door, I answered it, but no one was there. So I went back to blasting my stereo with my favorite songs by Sandi Patty. Yeah, we had cassette tapes back then, not playlists!

I heard more pounding on my door, but again, no one was there. I assumed some kids were playing pranks, but then I heard someone scream, "Get out! The building is on fire!" I ran outside to see ten-foot flames shooting out the kitchen window in the apartment next to mine. We shared a wall between our units. My neighbor on the other side ran back and forth between her apartment and the curb with a laundry basket full of stuff. She had whacked my door each time she ran back into her apartment for another armload. She was trying to warn me while grabbing as much stuff as she could. Finally, I registered the siren in the background. (I really should listen to my music with a little less volume.)

Some firemen appeared and ordered everyone to evacuate. I had no time to grab anything. The firemen quickly escorted my neighbor and me across the street. They would not allow us back inside our homes. My other neighbor, whose apartment was now engulfed with flames, stood there sobbing.

Throngs of people had gathered from every direction when I heard a fireman yell to another, "We can't save this one. Just keep it from spreading to the other buildings." I sat on the curb and contemplated the odds of one person losing everything twice, and before the age of twenty! When I was eight, my family moved from Arkansas to California, and our moving truck was stolen. Everything we owned was gone in an instant. Now my home stood surrounded by flames. Could this really be happening again?

The words of Job 1:21 came to mind: "Naked I came from my mother's womb, and naked I will leave this life. The LORD gives, and the LORD takes away. Praise the name of Yahweh." The smoke filled my nostrils as I thought about my youth pastor's wife, Kandee. When I spilled grape soda on her new white carpet, she said to me, "Please, don't give it another thought. I wasn't planning on taking that carpet with me to heaven anyway." I sat on the curb and exhaled. And a peace that can only be described as surpassing all human understanding came over me. I prayed for my neighbors while I watched the fire advance like tendrils, twisting around each banister and rail.

The firemen tore holes in the second-story roof and aimed their hoses. Eventually, they quelled the spreading destruction. Several neighbors lost everything to ashes while the rest had varying degrees of smoke and water damage. To everyone's surprise, my apartment, opposite the wall where the fire started, was the only unit unscathed.

Sometimes it seems there's no rhyme or reason as to why some things happen. One moment, we lose everything. Another moment, we escape ruin. Why did God allow our moving truck to be stolen? Why did He allow my apartment to remain intact? I don't know. But I do know I share Paul's heart when he says, "I know what it is to be in need, and I know what it is to have plenty. I have learned the secret of being content in any and every situation, whether well fed or hungry, whether living in plenty or in want" (4:12 NIV). This is another step toward living a life of deeper joy: learning to be content with a little or a lot.

Read Philippians 4:10-14

Paul's hardships are well documented. He's been beaten and imprisoned. Starved and stoned. Shipwrecked and left in the open sea (see 2 Corinthians

6:3-10). And yet he experiences joy in spite of his suffering. Paul sounds like Superman, but he isn't. He'd be the first to admit it too. Paul isn't superhuman, but he does experience supernatural power because Christ lives in him. That's what he means when he says, "I am able to do all things through Him who strengthens me" (4:13). Paul isn't the only one either. The same Jesus who strengthens Paul to overcome all adversity strengthens us too! We aren't superhuman, but the supernatural power of the Holy Spirit lives inside us. We, too, can do all things through the power of Jesus Christ.

> We aren't superhuman, but the supernatural power of the Holy Spirit lives inside us.
>
> #WordWriters

Diving Deeper

What is Paul referring to in verse 10 when he says, "Once again you renewed your care for me"?

What is Paul's secret for being content? Is this secret for being content available to you too?

What does it mean that you can do all things through Christ who strengthens you?

Write out Philippians 4:10-14, thanking God for enabling us to face whatever challenges may come our way.

Prayer: Thank You, Lord, that genuine contentment is never out of the realm of possibility. With You all things are possible. Even contentment! Forgive me when I settle for a discontented heart. Help me to remember that all these earthly things dim in the light of Your goodness to me. Amen.

The Joy of Secret Giving

Open my eyes so that I may contemplate wonderful things from Your instruction.

PSALM 119:18

My Grandma Lucy used to call her couch a "davenport," and she had a handmade blue-and-white quilt draped over the back of it. I loved that quilt. I used to lie on her davenport and trace my fingers over the intricate designs, following the stitches in loops. For as long as I can remember, I wanted to learn how to quilt, but it seemed too complicated. So I settled for being an admirer of the craft.

One day I walked past a quilt store, and I stopped to ooh and aah over the quilts in the window. A sign in the corner caught my eye. A beginner's class was starting the following Wednesday. No previous quilting experience was required. I walked into the store to learn more about the class, and to my own surprise, I walked out of the store having signed up for the class. That serendipitous walk past the quilt shop marked a significant beginning for me.

I spent the next five years taking one quilting class after another. My kids were babies and toddlers at the time, so this was my one night a week to do something fun, just for me. I discovered a whole network of quilting stores in Southern California, and I'd visit a new store once or twice a month. I was always working on a project, so new fabric was always required! A dear friend at my husband's workplace helped me figure out my new sewing machine, and she invited me to her quilting circle.

My first night at the quilting circle was delightful. The women met once a month and they heartily welcomed me in. I grew to love these women as much as I loved the craft. I learned the names of their children and grandchildren, and they learned the names of my kids. We were all fast friends. And whenever I was stumped with a project, they taught me their favorite sewing tricks.

When the 2008 recession affected households across America, my husband's workplace went through several rounds of downsizing and the remaining employees experienced some degree of income reduction. As a result, we needed to reassess our spending and saving habits. Needless to say, my quilting hobby was one of the things we had to cut from our monthly budget. I know it's not a big deal in the grand scheme of things; we knew many who lost their jobs and their homes. So we were grateful to be making ends meet, but all the discretionary spending—like buying fabric for a quilt project—was over.

For a while, I continued to attend my monthly sewing group and appreciate the wonderful creations my friends shared, but I stopped taking projects of my own. Eventually, I stopped going. I explained that quilting wasn't something I could reasonably afford anymore—at least not in this season of life. They all graciously understood.

A few weeks later, a sewing buddy called and asked if she could drop by my house. Upon her arrival, she greeted me with a big hug and big mystery bag. She could barely contain her excitement as she ushered me to my dining room table to spill the contents of the bag. Color-coordinated fabric, matching thread, batting, and a pattern soon covered my table. She was careful to explain that the quilting kit wasn't from her but from my Secret Quilt-Fairy Godmother.

It wasn't my birthday. It wasn't Christmas. This was one of those unexpected gifts that take you completely by surprise. As a writer, I love piecing together words as much as I love piecing together fabric. Yet it's hard for me to put into words what this gift of generosity meant to me. In today's reading, Paul thanks the Philippians again for their gifts. Their generosity sustained his well-being at a vulnerable time in his life.

---------------- *Read Philippians 4:15-20* ----------------

Paul wraps up his letter the same way he started—by giving thanks. He thanks the Philippians for their generosity, but more than that, Paul appreciates the way their gifts demonstrate how deeply they care for him. The church in Philippi loves Paul. They're so grateful for the investment he made in their lives. And their gifts are but a small token of their thanks.

Before Paul signs his letter, he ends by praying one more promise of God over his friends: "And my God will supply all your needs according to His riches in glory in Christ Jesus" (4:19). This is a paramount step toward a life of deeper joy: praying the promises of God over others. Nothing knits our hearts together better than prayer. Paul knew it. And the Philippians knew it.

Whenever I finish a quilt, I give it a name. After spending hours joyfully cutting and sewing the lovely quilt kit from my Secret Quilt-Fairy Godmother, I named the quilt my Friendship Quilt, and it lies on my "davenport" the way my grandma used to lay a quilt over hers. It reminds me what friendship is really made of. It's made of shared interests and time together. But more than anything friendship is like a quilt; it takes the pieces of our lives and stitches them together with love to make something beautiful.

> Friendship is like a quilt; it takes the pieces of our lives and stitches them together with love to make something beautiful.
>
> #WordWriters

Diving Deeper

How many other churches supported Paul with financial gifts the way the Philippians did?

At what other time in Paul's life did the Philippians send him gifts?

What does God promise to supply for us?

Today let's write out Philippians 4:15-20, thanking God that He's faithful to supply our needs according to His riches in glory.

Prayer: Thank You, Lord, for promising to provide for us. You always know what I need more than I know myself. Help me to trust You when it seems my provisions are running low. Help me to look to You to provide my daily manna. Amen.

A Call to See Beyond
~ fledgling beginnings ~

Something inside every human soul makes us want to be part of something bigger than ourselves. But sometimes we miss that "something bigger" because we confuse it with the world's idea of what "big" is supposed to look like. Sometimes the really big thing looks really small. It might even look like a small group of women gathering to pray by the river. Let's not be quick to look past fledgling beginnings. Because we just never know what the God of the universe might have in store.

The Lydia Legacy

Open my eyes so that I may contemplate wonderful things from Your instruction.

PSALM 119:18

From Day 1, we've talked about what happens when women gather. When Lydia and her friends in Philippi surrendered their lives to Jesus, they made themselves willing vessels to be used by Him. God then used this small group of women to build not only the first church in their city, but also the first church in Europe! I call it the Lydia Legacy. It's what can happen when a few women come together for the sole purpose of praying, reading Scripture, and seeking God.

Women have continued to do this for centuries. They may not have their names inscribed in the Holy Bible, but their names are written in the book of life. These women have influenced other women within their sphere. Not through a formal mentor program, but through the actions of their daily lives.

I've shared several examples of "Lydias" who have made an impact on my own spiritual growth. Mrs. Larson opened her home to me and let me stay with her when I needed a place to live. Allison the props manager taught me what it looks like to serve with gladness in hidden ways. My youth pastor's wife, Kandee, showed me grace I didn't deserve. Diana has been like an adopted grandma to my kids. Carolyn encouraged me to begin writing devotions. Marci reminded me how powerful it is when we meditate and memorize God's Word. And my Secret Quilt-Fairy Godmother blessed me with a sweet gift just to say she was thinking of me.

> The joy of the Lord becomes our strength when our hearts have found a home in Jesus.
>
> #WordWriters

I'm deeply grateful for all the "Lydias" in my life, but my dearest Lydia will always be my grandma. Just as Timothy's Grandma Lois taught him the truth of Scripture, my Grandma Lucy showed me Jesus with the way she lived her life. I can't imagine my childhood without her influence.

Now it's our turn. We can become a Lydia to the women in our lives. We may not even realize when someone is watching us. But the more we become like Jesus, the more we'll shine like stars, the way Paul describes it in Philippians 2:15. We don't have to try to shine, either. We simply need to look more like Him.

Read Philippians 4:21-23

The next time you attend church on a Sunday morning. Or the next time you attend a kid's soccer game on a Saturday afternoon. Or the next time you walk down a store aisle on a Tuesday evening. Remember, women are everywhere, and they're longing for someone to show them Jesus. Not in an overbearing way. Just in the way we go about our day. This is yet another way we can cultivate a life of deeper joy: shining with the love of Christ. For it's impossible to shine with the love of Christ while simultaneously nursing a grudge. God's love for us becomes His joy in us. The joy of the Lord becomes our strength when our hearts have found a home in Jesus.

Diving Deeper

Paul makes sure to tell the Philippians that even "those from Caesar's household" greet them. Why do you think Paul does this?

What are some of your takeaways from your time in Philippians?

How has writing the Word impacted your study of the Bible and your time with God?

Write out the final words of Philippians in 4:21-23, asking God to help you become a Lydia in someone's life today.

Prayer: Thank You, Lord, for loving me so much that You want to live inside me. I pray my love for You continues to grow and that my life will shine with Your love wherever I go. May I always look to You as the source of my joy. For You are the reason I can live each day with a deep, abiding joy that sees beyond the here-and-now. Amen.

Steps Toward a Life of Deeper Joy

Word Writers: Philippians

Day 1 – **Step 1:** Participating in a community of believers.

Day 2 – **Step 2:** Remembering with gratitude.

Day 3 – **Step 3:** Growing in love for one another.

Day 4 – **Step 4:** Accepting the limits of our situations.

Day 5 – **Step 5:** Rejoicing over the success of others.

Day 6 – **Step 6:** Finishing each season of life in a way that honors others.

Day 7 – **Step 7:** Living in harmony with others.

Day 8 – **Step 8:** Looking to the interests of others.

Day 9 – **Step 9:** Sacrificing for the sake of others.

Day 10 – **Step 10:** Committing Scripture to memory.

Day 11 – **Step 11:** Serving in hidden ways.

Day 12 – **Step 12:** Being at peace with whatever direction life takes.

Day 13 – **Step 13:** Investing in the life of another person.

Day 14 – **Step 14:** Honoring men and women who serve.

Day 15 – Step 15: Stepping into the calling God has placed on our lives.

Day 16 – Step 16: Building a life of great character.

Day 17 – Step 17: Waiting on God until He makes all things right again.

Day 18 – Step 18: Leaving our past in the past.

Day 19 – Step 19: Knowing that one day our bodies will be made whole.

Day 20 – Step 20: Handling conflict with humility, grace, and wisdom.

Day 21 – Step 21: Dwelling only on things that are true and good and beautiful.

Day 22 – Step 22: Learning to be content with a little or a lot.

Day 23 – Step 23: Praying the promises of God over others.

Day 24 – Step 24: Shining with the love of Christ.

Word Writers

Your Turn!

As you begin this journey of writing the Word,
I pray the truth and beauty of Scripture will be inscribed
on the tablet of your heart, drawing you nearer to Him.

~ Denise

Philippians

Philippians

Philippians

Philippians

Philippians

Philippians

Philippians

Philippians

Philippians

Philippians

Philippians _____

Philippians

Philippians

Philippians

Philippians _____

Philippians _____

Philippians _____

Philippians

Philippians _____

Philippians

Philippians

Philippians _____

Philippians _____

Philippians

Philippians

Philippians _____

Philippians

Philippians

Philippians

Philippians

Philippians

Philippians

Philippians

Philippians

Philippians

Philippians

Philippians

Philippians

Philippians

Philippians

Philippians

_____

_____

_____

_____

_____

_____

_____

_____

_____

_____

_____

_____

_____

_____

_____

_____

_____

Philippians

Philippians

Philippians

Philippians

Philippians

Philippians

Philippians _____

_____

_____

_____

_____

_____

_____

_____

_____

_____

_____

_____

_____

_____

_____

_____

Philippians _____

Philippians

Also from Denise J. Hughes

Relationship Wisdom... Handwritten on Your Heart

The book of Ephesians calls you to carry on with a rich understanding of God's love and the strength to serve those around you. Get ready to explore this magnificent book through the tried-and-tested inductive study method—with an added writing step to help you treasure each word!

As you dive into Ephesians you will learn how God intends for you to walk in His love and power, daily drawing closer to Him.

The Word Writers series helps you experience Scripture in a deeper way—on your own or with a group—through studying and writing verses word by word.